"ONE OF THE MANY THINGS I appreciate about Anne Barbour is that when she writes a lyric her thoughts are centered on the Lord Jesus Christ. She and her husband John, both accomplished musical artists and songwriters, have toured with me around the world for over 30 years and I am grateful for their partnership in the ministry of the Gospel.

As Anne put the finishing touches on this book, a debate raged about "what is the essential," and she answers the question in the title of her book *The Savior Has Come*. The *tinsel and glitter* of Christmas is nothing compared to the *truth and glory* of the Babe in the manger who came long ago. This book will cause you to remember Jesus' birth, reflect on his perfect life and miraculous resurrection, and anticipate Christ Jesus who is coming again soon.

– FRANKLIN GRAHAM
President and CEO, Samaritan's Purse
Billy Graham Evangelical Association

The SAVIOR HAS COME

𝒯ʰᵉ SAVIOR HAS COME

An Advent Devotional

ANNE BARBOUR

CENTENNIAL, COLO.

Printed in the United States of America

Unless otherwise indicated, Scripture quotations are from the ESV® Bible
(The Holy Bible, English Standard Version®), copyright © 2001 by Crossway.
Used by permission. All rights reserved.

O Come Let Us Adore Him
C. Frederick Oakeley | John Francis Wade
© Words: Public Domain

FaithHappenings Publishing
A division of WordServe Literary
7500 E. Arapahoe Rd., Suite 285 • Centennial, CO 80112
admin@wordserveliterary.com • 303.471.6675

Cover Design: Francine Eden Platt • Eden Graphics, Inc.
Cover Photo: Joanna Malinowska • freestocks.org
Interior Book Design: Francine Eden Platt • Eden Graphics, Inc.
Interior Photos: stock.adobe.com and istockphoto.com

Bio Photo: Kevin Caldwell
© 2014 Copyright Off the Rails Australasia Pty Ltd/Used with permission

ISBN: 978-1-941555-44-6

Second Printing, August 2021

~ For Evan ~

Courageous, resilient, resolved.
You will forever inspire me.

Love, Mom

Introduction

WHILE THE SHELVES of shops are stocked with all things Christmas long before the season arrives, this writer chooses to begin her Advent reflections at the start of the month of December. It has been my personal preference that December 1 officially launch Christmastime. I'm reluctant to move too quickly out of the sweetness of the celebration of Thanksgiving. And that makes this Advent devotional a little unique, forgoing the traditional "fourth Sunday before Christmas" start. Allow yourself to linger a little while longer in the spirit of gratitude that celebrating Thanksgiving brings.

As I wrote these entries, I found myself encountering not the details of the story of Jesus' birth, but Jesus Himself. That was wonderfully unexpected and became my first and best gift of Christmas. I am praying something similar will happen for you as you enter familiar terrain. If you ask Jesus for that first gift of Christmas, I feel certain He will give it to you. I'm praying for you as you read, reflect, and listen for the sweet voice of the Savior of the world.

Hope OF THE PROMISED ONE
First Theme of Advent

Faith IN THE WAITING
Second Theme of Advent

Joy AT HIS COMING
Third Theme of Advent

Peace NOW AND FOREVER
Fourth Theme of Advent

My soul magnifies the Lord,
and my spirit rejoices in God my Savior.

~ LUKE 1:47

GUIDE to reading
The Savior Has Come

WELCOME TO *The Savior Has Come – Advent Devotional.*
Beginning on December 1, you will find an entry
for each day through Christmas Eve. The month is split
into four themes that follow a traditional Advent form—
HOPE, FAITH, JOY, and PEACE. Here is a short guide
to help you get the most out of your time with the Lord.

Meditation:

These passages from the Bible are here for reflection, providing opportunities for the Lord to give you a fresh look
at pieces of the story surrounding Jesus' birth. I encourage
you to linger in the passage, allowing your soul to settle in
the presence of God. There is so much treasure to be found
for those who will wait upon Him in this way, especially if
the passages of scripture are very familiar.

Reflection:

This section provides reflections from the daily passage. They are meant to ignite streams of thought as you remain in the presence of the Lord. You are encouraged to journal your own reflections so that you have a memory of the way God speaks to you during Advent.

Response:

The prayer provided is a launchpad into your own dialogue with God. I would encourage you to ask God to speak to you as you move through the business of your day. Enjoy His presence with you today as you remember who He is and the significance of His birth.

Remember:

This section provides you with an opportunity to jot down thoughts as you meditate, and reflect, and pray. In doing so you create a time capsule for the future which I pray will make this volume especially meaningful in the years to come. There are so many benefits to remembering how the Lord stirred our hearts and what it is He meant for us to pay attention to on a particular occasion.

Hope OF THE PROMISED ONE

First Theme of Advent

DECEMBER 2020 closes out a year that has been riddled with life-altering challenges. We do not yet know when the dust will settle, but we already find ourselves individually and collectively weary. It seems the moment we orient to significant changes, there is a new mandate or set of statistics that force change again.

COVID19, government mandates, racially motivated violence, rioting and looting, and a presidential election year are but a sampling of those hot-buttons that have wreaked havoc upon the world, upon the United States, and upon the family of God throughout the world. We are fighting to preserve unity among the global church so that we can be the haven so needed by troubled souls everywhere.

It is in this climate we find the need of hope to be more felt than perhaps at any time in the last half-century. Christ followers understand that hope is found in Jesus and in no one else. The one promised as the Savior of the world has come. And He's coming again! We celebrate Him and find our hope in Him as we remember the events of His blessed birth.

And now, O Lord, for what do I wait?

My hope is in you.

~ PSALM 39:7

BESIDES ME THERE IS
NO SAVIOR

Hope of The Promised One

Meditation:

"You are My witnesses," declares the Lord,
"and My servant whom I have chosen,
that you may know and believe Me
and understand that I am He.
Before Me no God was formed,
nor shall there be any after Me.
I, I am the Lord,
and besides Me there is no savior."

~ ISAIAH 43:10–11

Reflection:

The Christmas story exists because of humanity's need for a Savior. It is God's answer in response to that need. Christ entering the world through the womb of a virgin, invoking the glorious singing of hosts of angels, was the way in which God bridged the gap opened up because of our sin. This plan was put into place from eternity. It was not the Godhead's top pick from a list of possibilities. It was the only way in which we would be able to reestablish relationship with our Maker. So for many, many generations, faithful men and women hoped and waited for the coming of this Promised One.

The birth of our Savior is one in a glorious sequence of historical events that reveal the radical love God has for humanity. There is not a person walking the planet who does not experience the overflow of that love. But benefiting from the love of God is not the same thing as embracing God's gift to us through the life, death, resurrection, and ascension of Jesus Christ. That comes through faith in Jesus and the surrendering of ourselves to His Lordship. Is Jesus Lord of your life? If He is, you are among the multitude of witnesses who testify that the Christ Child is, in fact, the Savior of the world! As Christmas approaches may we seize every opportunity to point people to the only One who can save them!

Response:

Lord, I draw near to You as I will for the next several weeks to ponder the miracle of the birth of Jesus. Thank You for sending Your Son into the world to save! Speak to me about things I don't yet understand. Waken in me a deeper passion for You that I didn't know I could have. You have gone to unimaginable lengths to save my life! Help that reality inform my responses to all that happens today. And please, Lord, may I be a witness who declares without hesitation that life is found in You and You alone.

Remember:

_____

_____

_____

_____

_____

_____

_____

_____

_____

_____

OUR NEED FOR HOPE

Hope of The Promised One

Meditation:

Praise is due to You, O God, in Zion,
and to You shall vows be performed.
O You who hear prayer, to You shall all flesh come.
By awesome deeds You answer us with righteousness,
O God of our salvation, the hope
of all the ends of the earth.

~ PSALM 65: 1–2;5

Reflection:

Have you ever thought that before Eve "took of its fruit and ate" (Genesis 3:6), there was no need for hope? Eden was home. The earth was ruled by Adam and Eve on God's behalf, and they had direct access to God. It was a perfect existence! But Adam and Eve's willful decision was about to put all of humanity at odds with God. There would be nothing we could do to remedy this terrible new reality. We now desperately needed hope, and God had no intention of leaving us without it.

The Story of Christmas is the story of the One who would be the hope of all the ends of the earth. Many

Biblical scholars believe God inferred as much when He addressed the serpent in Genesis 3:15. The need had only just presented itself, and God was foreshadowing what He intended to do about it!

God didn't scramble for a response to our sin. He set in motion a remedy He had established from eternity. That's supposed to blow our minds! The fall of humanity did not catch God off His game! The Christ Child was always going to be the one who would deliver us from death and bring us hope.

Response:

Lord, thank You for knowing from eternity what it is I would need and for planning for it before the need ever arose. Thank You for putting the remedy in place. Thank You for giving me hope though the arrival of the Christ Child. Grow in me a sense of anticipation as Christmas approaches! Thank You for being my salvation and my hope! Help me to put that hope on display as I live out the day before me!

Remember:

_____

_____

_____

THE CHRIST CHILD —
RIGHT ON TIME

Hope of The Promised One

Meditation:

When the fullness of time had come,
God sent forth His Son,
born of woman, born under the law,
to redeem those who were under the law,
so that we might receive adoption as sons.
And because you are sons,
God has sent the Spirit of His Son into
our hearts, crying, "Abba! Father!"
So you are no longer a slave, but a son,
and if a son, then an heir through God.

~ GALATIANS 4:4–7

Reflection:

About 2,600 years ago, the angel Gabriel visited the prophet Daniel and prophesied concerning "the coming of an anointed one, a prince" (Daniel 7:24). This Chosen One would enter the world to bring about our redemption. But when would this take place? Daniel had been desperately crying out to the Lord for mercy and forgiveness for

God's people. I wonder how he would have felt to know six hundred years would pass before the Anointed One would come?

When the Prince of Peace did arrive, He entered the world not a moment late . . . but not one second early. God's flawless plan would be carried out just as it was designed to, to a fraction of a second. The timing of God has been contemplated by many down through the ages. We too are meant to marvel at the perfection of God's timing. It ought to encourage us as we wait upon God for things we are crying out to Him for. He hears and responds in perfect time just like He always has!

Response:

Lord, as I move another day closer to celebrating the birth of Jesus, I'm awestruck by the beauty of Your perfection. You are perfect, and all You do is perfect. Thank you for the gift of the Christ Child who came at just the right moment in human history. Your plans for me are also perfect, and I can be hope-filled even as I wait upon You. Let the gratitude and wonder I feel right now follow me through this day so that others might see . . . there is hope for those who wait upon the Lord!

Remember:

_____

_____

_____

_____

_____

_____

_____

_____

_____

THE CHRIST CHILD –
THE LAMB THAT WAS SLAIN

Hope of The Promised One

Meditation:

Behold the lamb of God,
who takes away the sins of the world.

~ JOHN 1:29

You were ransomed from the futile ways
inherited from your forefathers,
not with perishable things such as silver or gold,
but with the precious blood of Christ,
like that of a lamb without blemish or spot.

~ 1 PETER 1:18

Reflection:

In twenty days, we will celebrate the arrival of Immanuel, God with us. For all the wonder within me as I "peer" into the manger at the Christ Child, I can't help but see the One who would become the Lamb who was slain for the sins of the world. There is a mixture of joy and sorrow… and then joy again as I recall all that would take place over the next thirty-three years of Jesus' life on earth.

I believe it's healthy, even necessary, to remember the whole story at Christmas. It shouldn't rob us of the ability to celebrate whole-heartedly the wonder that God entered the world as an infant. At the same time, our hearts should be deeply impacted by the reason He came. It was not to inaugurate an annual gift-giving holiday, but to fulfill the crippling debt against humanity because of our sin. He paid that debt in full by giving His life as a ransom for many (Mark 10:45).

Response:

Lord, You were the Babe in the manger… AND You are the Lamb of God, who came to take my sin upon Yourself and ransom my life. There is no adequate way to say thank You. My life belongs to You because You purchased it with Your precious blood. How do You want me to think and feel as I move a day closer to Christmas? How can I hold the tensions inherent in Your story so that You receive the glory You are due? Let the joy of Christmas abound in me, and let the costly price that Babe in the manger would pay keep me humble and deeply grateful.

Remember:

_____

_____

THE CHRIST CHILD –
SON OF MAN

Hope of The Promised One

Meditation:

For as Jonah became a sign to the people of Nineveh,
so will the Son of Man be to this generation.

~ LUKE 11:30

The Son of Man came not to be served but to serve,
and to give his life as a ransom for many."

~ MATTHEW 20:28

Reflection:

Jesus referred to Himself most often as the Son of Man. What was He trying to tell us by using that title time and again? Only a man without blemish or spot could be offered as an acceptable sacrifice for the sins of humankind (1 Peter 1:19). And of course, no ordinary human had or would ever live a sinless life. So God, driven by His love for us, saw fit to send His Son to earth to be born in the likeness of man (Philippians 2:7).

Jesus went out of His way to identify with us even in

the title He most often chose for Himself. The birth of Jesus was the birth of the Son of Man. There in the manger lay the fulfillment of the vision given to the prophet Daniel some six hundred years before:

> and behold, with the clouds of heaven
> there came one like a Son of Man,
> and He came to the Ancient of Days
> and was presented before Him.
> And to Him was given dominion
> and glory and a kingdom,
> that all peoples, nations,
> and languages should serve Him;
> His dominion is an everlasting dominion,
> which shall not pass away,
> and His kingdom one that shall not
> be destroyed (Daniel 7:13-14).

Response:

There are so many names given to You throughout Your Word. That You would identify with me as the Son of Man is something I don't pretend to comprehend. But I'm in awe of You, sinless Son of Man. All praise to You Jesus —the One who has been given the name above every other name!

Remember:

_____

_____

_____

_____

_____

_____

_____

_____

_____

THE CHRIST CHILD – SON OF GOD

Hope of The Promised One

Meditation:

The Lord said to me, "You are my Son;
today I have begotten You.
Ask of Me, and I will make the nations Your heritage,
and the ends of the earth Your possession.

~ PSALM 2:7–8

And a voice came from heaven,
"You are My beloved Son; with You I am well pleased."

~ MARK 1:11

Reflection:

We close the first theme of Advent by drawing our attention to another title given to Jesus. Sixty-seven times in the New Testament Jesus is referred to as the Son of God. The Babe in the manger was the Son of God. Our natural mind rejects such an implausibility. But an over-familiarity with the title Son of God might cause us to skip over the wondrous fact: God's Son, a member of the Godhead, once laid in a manger as a baby boy! Selah (pause and reflect)!

Imagine being present and peering into the manger where the infant Jesus lay. And imagine declaring these words of truth as you looked upon Him: "And we know that the Son of God has come and has given us understanding, so that we may know Him who is true; and we are in Him who is true, in His Son Jesus Christ. He is the true God and eternal life" (1 John 5:20).

The Christ Child is none other than the Son of God. He was begotten of the Father from eternity which means He has no beginning. He is God. He is God the Son, a distinct person from the Father and the Spirit, but one in essence with them! And a few thousand years ago, He lay in a manger as a helpless Babe.

Response:

I worship You, Son of God. You are fully God... as is the Father... as is the Spirit. You convened as the Triune Being and mapped out the way You would ransom humanity. You ransomed me! My heart is overflowing with awe and wonder and gratitude! Thank You, Lord! You do all things well. Thank you for the HOPE I have in You... the Promised One... the Son of God... my Redeemer and Savior!

Remember:

_____

_____

_____

_____

_____

_____

_____

_____

_____

Faith IN THE WAITING

Second Theme of Advent

"N ow FAITH is the assurance of things hoped for, the conviction of things not seen. For by it the people of old received their commendation," (Hebrews 11:1-2). The entries for our second theme remind us of the platform that hope can be to help launch and sustain our faith. Faith grows in an environment of hope, so it's a wonderful trait to consider on the heels of our look at hope found in the Christmas story.

Christians are to be people of unwavering faith in God and in His promises. But sometimes faith weakens as we battle invitations to be afraid. The world around us is profoundly troubled and fearful, and, frankly, it's understandable. The six people we will look at over the next six days will remind us what assurance in the promises of God looks like. They remind us what conviction in the face of opposition and implausible circumstances looks like. These courageous, godly men and women are meant to show us the way through adversity. We need their stories of faith as never before.

Then He touched their eyes, saying,
"According to your faith be it done to you."

~ MATTHEW 9:29

THE FORERUNNER –
JOHN THE BAPTIST

Faith In The Waiting

Meditation:

Behold, I send my messenger,
and he will prepare the way before Me.

~ MALACHI 3:1

A voice cries: "In the wilderness prepare
the way of the Lord; make straight in the desert
a highway for our God."

~ ISAIAH 40:3

There was a man sent from God, whose name was John.
He came as a witness, to bear witness about the light.

~ JOHN 1:6–7

He will be filled with the Holy Spirit,
even from his mother's womb.
And he will turn many of the children of Israel
to the Lord their God.

~ LUKE 1:15–16

Reflection:

Our second theme of Advent will focus on a few primary figures surrounding the birth of Jesus. Each was invited by God to play very different but vital roles in the story of the coming Savior. We begin with the forerunner, John the Baptist. He shows up in the Christmas story as a Spirit-filled baby in utero who leaped in his mother's womb when the unborn Jesus was near him. Before he was even born, he was bearing witness that the Promised One had come!

The forerunner for the Savior of the world was strikingly humble: "The friend of the bridegroom rejoices greatly at the bridegroom's voice. Therefore this joy of mine is now complete. He must increase, but I must decrease," (John 3:29-30). His was a humility akin to that of Jesus. John also possessed an unshakable clarity of purpose: "I am the voice of one crying out in the wilderness, make straight the way of the Lord" (John 1:23).

How utterly Christ-like, never to put yourself forward, but to live to elevate Jesus! And how fulfilling to be so clear about who you are and why you're walking the earth that you confidently live it out! John lived his life under the sway of God the Spirit. It shouldn't surprise us, then, that he would so profoundly emulate the One he was born to usher in! May God have access to our hearts, so that we represent Him to those in our path as John did… humbly and without reservation.

Response:

Lord, I'm inspired by the clarity and resolve of John the Baptist. And I'm convicted by the depth of his humility. Please use this time of remembering the birth of Jesus to make me the person You would have me be for Your glory! Capture my heart and be the ruling force within me. Help me to boldly yet humbly declare the truth about the Babe in the manger who is Christ the Lord!

Remember:

_____

_____

_____

_____

_____

_____

_____

_____

_____

Elizabeth – Mother of John the Baptist

Faith In The Waiting

Meditation:

> And they [Zechariah and Elizabeth]
> were both righteous before God,
> walking blamelessly in all the commandments
> and statutes of the Lord.
>
> ~ LUKE 1:6

> And when Elizabeth heard the greeting of Mary,
> the baby leaped in her womb.
> And Elizabeth was filled with the Holy Spirit,
> and she exclaimed with a loud cry,
> "Blessed are you among women,
> and blessed is the fruit of your womb!
> And why is this granted to me that the mother
> of my Lord should come to me?
> For behold, when the sound of your greeting
> came to my ears,
> the baby in my womb leaped for joy.
> And blessed is she who believed
> that there would be a fulfillment of what
> was spoken to her from the Lord."
>
> ~ LUKE 1:41–45

Reflection:

The mother of John the Baptist may be on my top-five list of people I can't wait to meet in heaven. So much about Elizabeth's character and enthusiasm is revealed in the brief text above. It's enough for her to be seen as a person any of us would be honored to emulate. Like her son would be, Elizabeth was remarkably in tune with what was happening within her and around her. The righteousness she displayed in her life before her pregnancy was equally present after… as the miracles began to flow! She was just amazing.

Unlike her poor hubby, Elizabeth didn't seem to struggle to receive the news that the angel Gabriel delivered. She thanked God and recognized the favor He extended to her by removing her reproach as a barren woman and granting her the honor of being in the presence of the unborn Messiah. She was also an agent of encouragement for Mary, quick to applaud Mary for her great faith! Oh, to be like Elizabeth!

Response:

Lord, I want to have the awareness of Elizabeth especially as Christmas approaches. Sensitize my spirit by Your Spirit, so that I'm quick to see You at work and give You honor. Let me be unashamed and generous in my praise of You, and let it be contagious, just as Elizabeth's testimony is to me! Thank you for her life and for the gift it has been for two thousand years.

Remember:

_____

_____

_____

_____

_____

_____

_____

_____

Joseph –
A Man of Character

Faith In The Waiting

Meditation:

Now the birth of Jesus Christ took place in this way.
When his mother Mary had been betrothed to Joseph,
before they came together she was found to be with
child from the Holy Spirit. And her husband Joseph, being
a just man and unwilling to put her to shame, resolved
to divorce her quietly. But as he considered these things,
behold, an angel of the Lord appeared to him in a dream,
saying, "Joseph, son of David, do not fear to take Mary as
your wife, for that which is conceived in her is from the
Holy Spirit. She will bear a son, and you shall call his name
Jesus, for he will save his people from their sins."
When Joseph woke from sleep, he did as the angel
of the Lord commanded him: he took his wife,
but knew her not until she had given birth to a son.
And he called His name Jesus.

~ MATTHEW 1:18–21; 24–25

Reflection:

The story of Joseph is a study in godly character. God hand-picked Joseph to do what only a man of godly character could do. The short text above reveals an amazing look into Joseph's remarkable nature. I believe God would have these traits come to bear in all His sons and daughters.

As I've meditated on the passage above, here is what comes to the fore.

Joseph was—

just — He cared about what was right.

kind — He cared about not bringing shame.

wise — He weighed the variables and made a plan he was resolved to carry out.

thoughtful — He paused to think and ponder, even after he was resolved.

tempered — He was afraid, but fear didn't drive his actions.

teachable — He was open to hear from God.

obedient — Once God spoke, it was a done deal. He acted immediately.

disciplined — He waited to consummate his marriage.

What would it look like for you and me to approach today with the hope of exhibiting some of these beautiful qualities? It can happen if the Spirit has hold of our hearts! That's what made the difference for Joseph. Especially during a season where people might be sincerely wondering about the Babe in the manger, let's be approachable... resolved to put the character of our Lord on display.

Response:

Holy Spirit, walk me through this list of traits and speak to me about my own character... or lack of character. Thank You for Joseph. Thank You for telling me part of his story and giving me such an exceptional example of godliness. It helps me know how I'm meant to represent You to the world!

Remember:

_____

_____

_____

_____

_____

_____

_____

Mary – The Mother of Jesus

Faith In The Waiting

Meditation:

> Mary said, "Behold, I am the servant of the Lord;
> let it be to me according to your word."

~ LUKE 1:37

Reflection:

The angel Gabriel was really making the rounds in Luke's first chapter. His next proclamation would be for a teenage girl. Once again, he bore vital news that no other person in all of history would receive. Mary would be challenged as no one had ever been challenged. I cannot move past Mary's initial response (written above) to Gabriel. There is plenty here to provide us with the day's pondering.

Two things jump out of the text. Mary knew who she was "I am the servant of the Lord" therefore a hearty and quick "yes" was the only answer she would give "let it be to me according to your word." While she was naturally curious about how she could conceive a child (understatement of the ages), her "yes" did not hinge upon her ability to understand. It may be among the most profound examples of faith in all of Scripture.

Is that how you respond when God the Spirit speaks to you? Don't despair! We all have room to grow and much to learn from Mary. It couldn't hurt any of us to spend today meditating upon her simple faith-laden response to Gabriel.

Response:

Lord, today, as Christmas stands twelve days out, I stand in awe of this little girl and the godly wisdom she possessed. Thank You for a glimpse into her radical faith! It's jaw-dropping and convicting in the best sense of the word! Ground me in my identity and faith (like you did Mary) so that I answer "yes," no matter the challenge You put before me!

Remember:

_____

_____

_____

_____

_____

_____

SIMEON THE DEVOUT

Faith In The Waiting

Meditation:

Now there was a man in Jerusalem,
whose name was Simeon,
and this man was righteous and devout,
waiting for the consolation of Israel,
and the Holy Spirit was upon him.
And it had been revealed to him by the Holy Spirit
that he would not see death before
he had seen the Lord's Christ.
And he came in the Spirit into the temple,
and when the parents brought in the child Jesus,
to do for him according to the custom of the Law,
he took Him up in his arms and blessed God.

~ LUKE 2:25–27

Reflection:

I love Simeon's story, and I love the kind of person he represents. Even though God had been silent for several hundred years, devout men and women like Simeon faithfully waited and prayed for the Promised One to arrive. Tradition held that these precious few were known as the quiet of the land. How counter-cultural to be one of the quiet ones! The elderly Simeon was seen by God and was mightily rewarded. The Spirit sent him to the temple that day to see, carry, and bless the infant Jesus and his family. Just amazing!

Today, as we reflect, I wonder if we might examine our own resolve to faithfully pray and wait, not for the Babe in a manger, but for the returning King. What better time to renew our resolve than as Christmas approaches. May Simeon's story inspire us to do just that.

Response:

Lord, Simeon reminds me that Your eyes "run to and fro throughout the whole earth, to give strong support to those whose heart is blameless toward Him" (2 Chronicles 16:9). Thank you for righteous, devout Simeon and for stopping and fixing Your eyes upon him! You still look for the Simeons of the world… those who cling to Your promises and pray and wait for them to come to pass! Help me by Your Spirit to be among the quiet of the land.

Remember:

_____

_____

_____

ANNA THE PROPHETESS

Faith In The Waiting

Meditation:

And there was a prophetess, Anna,
the daughter of Phanuel, of the tribe of Asher.
She was advanced in years, having lived
with her husband seven years,
and then as a widow until she was eighty-four.
She did not depart from the temple, worshiping
with fasting and prayer night and day.
And coming up at that very hour
she began to give thanks to God
and to speak of Him to all who were
waiting for the redemption of Jerusalem.

~ LUKE 2: 36-38~

Reflection:

Eighty-four-year-old Anna would encounter the promised child moments after Simeon did. She too was among the quiet of the land and like Simeon, received the rare gift of bearing witness to the infant Jesus.

Anna's commitment to waiting well was utterly comprehensive. She would not leave the premises of the temple... not ever. How many eighty-four-year-olds (or anyone, for that matter) do you know who have zero moments to spare because of their sacrifice of worship, prayer, and fasting to the Lord? Do the math in the text above... Anna spent the bulk of her life demonstrating her radical commitment to God. She was one dedicated lady.

The story of waiting and waiting faithfully is a huge piece of the story of the birth of Jesus. I pray this week your soul has been reawakened to the quality of the people God chose to participate in the quiet entrance of Emmanuel! May their stories inspire and encourage us as we move another day closer to the celebration of His birth!

Response:

Lord, the stories of John the Baptist, Elizabeth, Joseph and Mary, and these precious elderly ones are such a gift. Help me by Your Spirit to move past the inspiration I feel so that You can work true transformation into me. I want to be found faithful as they were! And send me to people this Christmas season who need to know that the Christ Child came to earth for them.

Remember:

_____

_____

$\mathcal{Joy}$ AT HIS COMING

Third Theme of Advent

There were a select few who were poised to see and understand that the Babe in the manger was none other than the Son of God, come to save the world. I'm not sure it's possible to understand the euphoria they would have experienced as eye-witnesses to events people had been anticipating for centuries.

But joy awaits us too as we pause to remember the birth of Jesus. "And let them offer sacrifices of thanksgiving, and tell of His deeds in songs of joy" (Psalm 107:22). As we recount the miraculous details of Jesus' birth, we can take the psalmist's suggestion, giving thanks and recounting what took place in Bethlehem with great joy!

We, not unlike the angel of the Lord, find ourselves in

a hurting, fearful world with the very best of news. "Fear not, for behold, I bring you good news of great joy that will be for all the people" (Luke 2:10). The message we carry is for every person walking the planet. It is truth that sets captives free. And it produces joy like nothing else can!

These things I have spoken to you,
that My joy may be in you,
and that your joy may be full.

~ JOHN 15:11

BETHLEHEM – SET APART

Joy at His Coming

Meditation:

> Rachel died and was buried on the way
> to Ephrath (that is, Bethlehem).
>
> ~ GENESIS 35:19

> The man's name was Elimelek, his wife's name was Naomi.
> They were Ephrathites from Bethlehem, Judah.
>
> ~ RUTH 1:2

> The Lord said to Samuel, "How long will you
> mourn for Saul, since I have rejected him as king over
> Israel? Fill your horn with oil and be on your way;
> I am sending you to Jesse of Bethlehem. I have
> chosen one of his sons to be king."
> David went back and forth from Saul to
> tend his father's sheep at Bethlehem.
>
> ~ 1 SAMUEL 16:1; 17:15

> "But you, Bethlehem Ephrathah, though you are small
> among the clans of Judah, out of you will come for
> Me one who will be ruler over Israel, whose origins
> are from of old, from ancient times."
>
> ~ MICAH 5:2

Reflection:

Bethlehem was ground-zero for some significant pieces of history throughout the Old Testament. It was just a small town in Judah until God elevated it to prominence, using it as a backdrop that would ensure its celebrity status for the rest of time. It means "house of bread" aptly named as the place where the Bread of Life would come into the world. There is a beautiful continuity through the entire lineage of Jesus that's tied to Bethlehem. The texts written above reveal as much.

What I find remarkable in God's plan of redemption (particularly in the Christmas story), is that there is not one detail that is insignificant. That includes the little town that shows up periodically throughout God's whole narrative. Sometimes there is nothing short of priceless, hidden treasure in details that wouldn't ordinarily capture our attention. I believe God is eager to reveal those treasures if only we would linger in the story with Him.

Perhaps today you would linger in your remembrance of Bethlehem. Not because Bethlehem is a wonder in and of itself, but because God chose this place. Every person or place or thing that God chooses to be part of His great story, He chooses purposefully. And I believe no matter where we would stop within the story there's something to be learned about our great Savior. Look for Him as you meander through the streets of Bethlehem today.

Response:

Lord, most often I move through the Christmas story so quickly I miss the details. But this is Your grand story, and no detail should go unnoticed. Frankly, I move through the details of my own life too quickly too! Help me find treasures You've tucked away and saved for those who would not be in a hurry. I have an idea they are hidden right under my nose. I don't want to miss anything You have for me... and I'd like to be aware enough to help others find their own treasure!

Remember:

_____

_____

_____

_____

_____

_____

_____

_____

Magi – Seekers, Finders

Joy at His Coming

Meditation:

After Jesus was born in Bethlehem in Judea,
Magi from the east came to Jerusalem and asked,
"Where is the one who has been born king of the Jews?
We saw His star when it rose and have come to worship Him."
Then Herod called the Magi secretly and found out
from them the exact time the star had appeared.
He sent them to Bethlehem and said,
"Go and search carefully for the Child.
As soon as you find Him, report to me,
so that I too may go and worship Him."
After they had heard the king, they went on their way,
and the star they had seen when it rose went ahead of them
until it stopped over the place where the Child was.
When they saw the star, they were overjoyed.
On coming to the house,
they saw the Child with his mother Mary.
And having been warned in a dream
not to go back to Herod,
they returned to their country by another route.

~ MATTHEW 2:1–2;7–12

Reflection:

How is it that pagan "wise men" recognized the revelation of the star in the sky and knew exactly what it meant? We don't know the answer, but we do know they were eager to follow that star and pay homage to the promised King. Almost no one was actively looking for signs that would alert them of the birth of Jesus, but these magi were. There are always surprises within the workings of God... details that don't seem like they belong.

But today as we remember this piece of the Christmas story, we can't miss the fact that God was absolutely in charge of every person and detail associated with the coming of Jesus. Even folks like poor King Herod, who thought his crafty plan could eliminate the Christ Child, was on God's radar. Don't you find great comfort in the all-encompassing control of God? And, look, if God's people are asleep on the watch, aren't you glad He opens the door for true seekers (whoever they are) to enter the story?

Response:

Lord, thank You so much for the magi. I'm sorry Your own people were not more in tune and aware. But I'm so grateful that didn't stop You from moving forward with Your plans! Thank You for inviting the magi in to the timeline of the coming of Jesus. I pray I would learn from them and seek You as they did... with my whole heart! You promise that when I do, I will be found by You (Jeremiah 29:13). And in Your sweet presence is joy... to the full!

Remember:

_____

_____

_____

_____

_____

_____

_____

_____

_____

Jesus – Born of a Virgin

Joy at His Coming

Meditation:

Therefore the Lord himself will give you a sign:
The virgin will conceive and give birth to a Son,
and will call Him Immanuel.

~ ISAIAH 7:14

All this took place to fulfill what the Lord
had said through the prophet:
"The virgin will conceive and give birth to a Son,
and they will call Him Immanuel"
(which means "God with us").

~ MATTHEW 1:22–23

Reflection:

How was the Son of God going to enter the world as a human unless He was born of a human? There is plenty of mystery surrounding the ways of God, but Gabriel's words to Mary, "The Holy Spirit will come on you, and the power of the Most High will overshadow you" (Luke 1:35), rank right up there. Maybe it shouldn't surprise us that much. If God can call the whole of creation into being out of nothing, He can certainly bypass the reproductive process He invented.

God the Father entrusted the earthly fathering of Jesus to Joseph, but the Son of God was not going to come into the world having a biological father. Apparently it was going to take a God/man to accomplish what was needed in order to restore us to our Maker. So God, in an act of marvelous creativity, saw to it that Jesus would be born of a virgin. The Christmas story is packed with the miraculous. May God give us insight into His nature as we ponder the virgin birth of our Lord.

Response:

Lord, there is not a single detail of the events of the birth of Jesus that does not give me a peek into Your nature and character. Thank You for showing me who You are as I meditate on the wonder of the virgin birth. You are unlimited in Your power and creativity. You don't seem to be bound by the structures You created and that means You do things that sometimes leave me scratching my head. You have proved time and again that You are the God of the impossible. Praise You for Your "wondrous works to the children of man" (Psalm 107)!

Remember:

_____

_____

_____

_____

_____

_____

_____

_____

_____

JESUS – BORN IN A MANGER

Joy at His Coming

Meditation:

> The time came for her to give birth.
> And she gave birth to her firstborn Son
> and wrapped Him in swaddling cloths
> and laid Him in a manger, because
> there was no place for them in the inn.
>
> ~ LUKE 2:6–7

> For unto you is born this day in the
> city of David a Savior, who is Christ the Lord.
> And this will be a sign for you: you will find a Baby
> wrapped in swaddling cloths and lying in a manger.
>
> ~ LUKE 2:11–12

Reflection:

A manger? A feeding trough? What could possibly be the point of having the Incarnate Son of God laid in a feeding trough? The text above says it was to be a sign. The function of the manger in the storyline was to act as a sign, so those sent to find Him would know for certain it was Him. How many mangers in Bethlehem would be occupied by babies? Find an infant in a feeding trough and you've found your baby!

Was the manger in a stable? Some think not. It may have been in a lower section of the house of one of Joseph's relatives. It wouldn't have been uncommon to find a manger or two indoors to accommodate the animals during the cold. Still, this sure seems like it's a long way from the ideal resting place for the Promised One.

In the grand scheme (the part that trickles down to us) the manger reminds us of the inconceivably humble life the King of kings would live throughout His years on the earth. After all, "He humbled Himself by becoming obedient to the point of death, even death on a cross" (Philippians 2:8). As lowly as the manger was, it was not the lowest the Savior would go to pay our debt of sin.

Response:

Lord, my flesh winces at the thought of You in the manger. At the same, I am filled with awe as I picture You laying there. I'm not meant to feel sorry for the Christ Child, but to be filled with Joy as I contemplate the wonder of the details of my rescue… details You set in place! You came humbly when You had every right to enter with all the fanfare befitting the one true God. All praise and glory is Yours!

Remember:

_____

_____

_____

_____

_____

_____

_____

_____

_____

JESUS – THE ANGELS REJOICE

Joy at His Coming

Meditation:

And there appeared to him (Zechariah)
an angel of the Lord standing on
the right side of the altar of incense.
I am Gabriel. I stand in the presence of God,
and I was sent to speak to you
and to bring you this good news.

~ LUKE 1:11; 19

In the sixth month the angel Gabriel
was sent from God to a virgin
betrothed to a man whose name was Joseph,
of the house of David.
And he came to her and said, "Greetings,
O favored one, the Lord is with you!"

~ LUKE 1:26–28;

And suddenly there was with the angel
a multitude of the heavenly host praising God.

~ LUKE 2:13–14

Reflection:

What a role the angels played in the story of the coming of Jesus! The sacred tasks conducted by Gabriel and others were of paramount importance *and* a high honor. Both the angels and the recipients of their tidings were part of some of the most compelling moments in human history. The position the angels enjoyed before God remained the same after Jesus accomplished His mission, but *everything* changed for humanity! Even so, the angels' praise of God was so effusive, you would have thought all that happened was for them! Any chance they got to make much of God, they did so mightily.

We humans have much to learn from the way the angels worship. As we reflect upon them throughout the events of the birth of Jesus, I pray we would invite the Holy Spirit to teach us to worship God with more abandon. The angels were and are very clear about where all glory goes, and they give generously. As the beneficiaries of the life, death, and resurrection of Jesus, we ought to spend every ounce of passion ascribing worth to our God!

Response:

Lord, I pray that praise would be the dominating expression of my heart throughout this Christmas season! Help me, by Your Spirit, to take the angels' lead and worship You as never before! Let my praise and adoration be a witness to those I meet so that they inquire about the joy in my heart and about You, the sole object of my worship!

Remember:

_____

_____

_____

_____

_____

_____

_____

_____

_____

Jesus – The Worshiped One

Joy at His Coming

Meditation:

And in the same region there
were shepherds out in the field,
keeping watch over their flock by night.
And an angel of the Lord appeared to them,
and the glory of the Lord shone around them,
and they were filled with great fear.
And the angel said to them, "Fear not, for behold,
I bring you good news of great joy that
will be for all the people. For unto you is born this day
in the city of David a Savior, who is Christ the Lord.
And this will be a sign for you: you will find a Baby
wrapped in swaddling cloths and lying in a manger."
And suddenly there was with the angel a multitude of
the heavenly hostpraising God and saying,
"Glory to God in the highest, and on earth peace
among those with whom He is pleased!"
When the angels went away from them into heaven,
the shepherds said to one another,
"Let us go over to Bethlehem and see
this thing that has happened,
which the Lord has made known to us."
And they went with haste and found

Mary and Joseph, and the Baby lying in a manger.
And when they saw it, they made known the saying
that had been told them concerning this Child.
And all who heard it wondered at what the shepherds
told them. But Mary treasured up all these things,
pondering them in her heart.
And the shepherds returned, glorifying and praising God
for all they had heard and seen, as it had been told them.

~ LUKE 2:8-12

Reflection:

For the first time one of the Godhead was worshiped in human form! Oh, my word! There is just nowhere within the human psyche for this to sit, yet it happened. And who got invited to that event? I mean, who would have actually believed what they were seeing? God cherry-picked a handful of people with faith we can hardly comprehend and gave them a front-row seat to the entrance of Immanuel. And not incidentally, God the Spirit was present and active seeing to it that no one missed a cue.

But the truth is, while He might not be walking the earth like He did two thousand years ago, He is just as actively seeking those who would come to Him. That includes you and every person you are going to encounter as you go about your business today. The shepherds didn't stop worshiping God when they left the manger scene...

they told everyone they encountered what they'd witnessed! It's almost Christmas. Let's be open and eager to help people find their way to Christ the Lord by bearing witness to what He has done for us. Let's worship Him for all to see!

Response:

Lord, the joy that Mary, Joseph, and the shepherds experienced (not to mention the hosts of heaven) is the same joy that You would have me experience in my life! You are as real this moment as You were when You were lying in that manger. Put Your joy on display in me today for Your glory and as a witness to those who need Your salvation!

Remember:

_____

_____

_____

_____

_____

_____

_____

$\mathcal{P}$eace NOW AND FOREVER

Fourth Theme of Advent

P EACE is produced in an environment of trust. The heart of a man or woman who trusts steadfastly in the Lord is a heart at peace. In these days of unprecedented unrest, peace seems impossible to find, let alone possess. But Christ followers know better! We have in our grasp a treasure that keeps us steady regardless of the drastic changes taking place all around us.

The world is meant to see this steadiness— this peace in us. When they see it, they will marvel because the presence of it simply won't make any sense. And here is where we joyfully proclaim the good news! We are at peace with our Maker through faith in Jesus Christ. They too can be at peace with God.

For too many, Christmas in the Western world has ironically become a peace killer. The tradition of excessive gift-giving creates pressures that have nothing at all to do with remembering the birth of the Savior. Family traditions, however lovely, mean those without healthy families can feel desperately isolated. Let's do our best to reconnect with what Christmas is really about and invite others to do the same. After all, the Prince of Peace has come! Merry Christmas, Everyone!

The Lord sits enthroned over the flood;
the Lord sits enthroned as King forever.
May the Lord give strength to His people!
May the Lord bless His people with peace!

~ PSLAM 29:10-11

JESUS – PRINCE OF PEACE

Peace Now and Forever

Meditation:

And He shall stand and shepherd His flock
in the strength of the Lord,
in the majesty of the name of the Lord His God.
And they shall dwell secure, for now He shall be great
to the ends of the earth. And He shall be their peace.

~ MICAH 5:1–5

"For to us a Child is born, to us a Son is given;
and the government shall be upon His shoulder
and His name shall be called
Wonderful Counselor, Mighty God,
Everlasting Father, Prince of Peace."

~ ISAIAH 9:6

Reflection:

Peace is our final theme for this advent devotional. Who is this Prince of Peace, who gives peace to those who love Him? The Bible makes no mystery of it— Jesus is the Prince of Peace, come to rescue anyone who would embrace His gift of life. Christmastime is that occasion when even non-believers are apt to be familiar with someone called the Prince of Peace. What better time to be His ambassadors!

As I consider why it matters that I understand Jesus as the Prince of Peace I'm aware that He is offering me a glimpse of part of His nature. He is a peaceful God. He is Himself at peace. He is at peace within His triune self. The world He created and the humans He formed were initially and perfectly at peace. And when He comes to redeem and set right all that is corrupt, His kingdom will be a kingdom of peace. Those within His Kingdom will be a people at peace. How could it be otherwise?

As you and I consider the birth of Jesus, I pray He would show us anew the heart of peace He possesses. And I pray that as we "gaze" at the Babe in the manger, we would indeed see and rejoice at the sight of Him.

Response:

Jesus, I thank You for the peace I have in You. I thank You for the peace that lives in me because I belong to You. Thank You for drawing my heart to Yours and showing me my need of You. You are the Prince of Peace. There is no other! I praise You and worship You. I pray You would transform my eyes so that I never look upon any symbol of Christmas without remembering and thanking You, the Prince of Peace.

Remember:

_____

_____

_____

_____

_____

_____

_____

_____

_____

_____

Because of Jesus – Peace In Me

Peace Now and Forever

Meditation:

"Glory to God in the highest,
and on earth peace
among those with whom He is pleased!"

~ LUKE 2:14

Reflection:

Never in my lifetime has peace been so sought after or so elusive (depending on where you're looking for it). As a Christ follower, I believe unreservedly that peace is found in Christ alone. Jesus Christ is the source of peace and is Himself peace. And as I am one of His followers, you ought to recognize His peace in me.

Where did I get this peace? God gave it to me when I became a follower of Jesus Christ. It's one of many gifts He gives to His children (talk about an amazing Christmas present)! It's a deposit from Him that I can either draw upon or not, but it's there for me and there is no end to the supply of it. I've been reminded anew that peace is not the absence of difficulty, but a gift that comes to bear in the midst of hardship. It acts as a steadying agent. It is used to keep me upright when a storm would topple me, and it bears clarifying: this is God's peace in me.

Are you at peace? You can be. You can know the Prince of Peace. It's His highest desire that you would enter into a relationship with Him through faith in Jesus Christ. What better time than Christmastime to make Jesus the Lord of your life. When you do that, you will receive the peace of God. It passes understanding. You will have it when all the circumstances of life say that you could not possibly be at peace. Ask Jesus today— *"Be Lord of my life!"*

Response:

Lord, You deposited PEACE in me the moment I made you Lord of my life. This year has been so challenging. Christmas has its own challenges that stand ready to rob me of this precious treasure. Help me today to do my part in drawing upon the peace You have given to me. Thank you, Prince of Peace! Thank you for the gift of peace!

Remember:

_____

_____

_____

BECAUSE OF JESUS –
PEACE ON ME

Peace Now and Forever

Meditation:

"But the fruit of the Spirit is love, joy,
peace, patience, kindness,
goodness, faithfulness, gentleness, self-control;
against such things there is no law.

~ GALATIANS 5:22

Reflection:

Peace is a fruit of the Spirit of God. Seem like an odd thing to think about at Christmas? In light of our Prince of Peace, there couldn't be a better time to consider that because of Jesus, I can bear this life-giving fruit. I'm actually meant to have branches laden with it! This is not ornamental fruit. It's supposed to do what fruit does— feed and nourish hungry people, and that means the people you meet as you go about your day today. If they are in need and hungry for peace, they are supposed to be able to find it in you in abundance. It is God's peace you would be giving them—produced by God the Spirit.

As you go about your day and encounter evidence of the approaching holiday, remember that people are literally starving spiritually. They need peace and are likely trying to find it any way they can. It's an amazing privilege to have your tree branches full and within reach, and then be used by God to help someone else. Am I supposed to enjoy God's peace in me? Of course. But God's peace is not just to be found in me. It's meant to be ON me, too!

Response:

Prince of Peace, You put Your peace inside of me. It steadies me no matter what is around me. But you also mean to feed people through me. What an honor! Please put people in my path today who are hungry and feed them Your peace. Praise You, Jesus! You are the reason I have peace. You are the reason anyone is able to find peace. Let the branches of my life be overflowing with peace, especially as the celebration of Your birth draws near!

Remember:

_____

_____

_____

_____

BECAUSE OF JESUS – PEACE FROM ME

Peace Now and Forever

Meditation:

"Therefore, since we have been justified by faith,
we have peace with God through our Lord Jesus Christ"

~ ROMANS 5:1

Reflection:

Because I belong to the Prince of Peace, I am called to be a peacemaker. I am at PEACE with God through faith in Christ, wearing His gospel of peace like shoes on my feet that go wherever I go. I am never more like a Child of God than when I am an agent of the gospel of His peace. I am never more like Jesus than when I am proclaiming the VERY good news that peace with God is possible for anyone who would put their trust in Him. I am God's emissary, charged and equipped to herald the good news, just as the angels did when they spoke to the shepherds in the fields outside Bethlehem.

The Prince of Peace offers peace. So does the world. Jesus is keen that I understand there is no comparison whatsoever between these two kinds of peace. Only *His* peace anchors the soul, steadying it regardless of how tumultuous and uncertain life becomes. It's Christmas. There is no better entrance into a conversation about the baby in the manger than right now. We have the high honor and binding responsibility to proclaim the gospel of peace to any who would listen!

Response:

Lord, Prince of Peace, peace is meant to be in me. It's meant to be on me as fruit is on a tree. It's meant to go forth from me as I proclaim the gospel of Your peace. Put me to work on behalf of your Kingdom so that others can find peace with God as I have. This is a work of Your Holy Spirit, but I can be an agent of delivery! Would You use me to that end today, Lord? I praise You and thank You for the honor of bearing Your name and sharing the very good news!

Remember:

_____

_____

_____

_____

The New Covenant

Peace Now and Forever

Meditation:

"Behold, the days are coming, declares the Lord,
when I will make a new covenant with the house of Israel
and the house of Judah, not like the covenant that I made
with their fathers on the day when I took them by the hand
to bring them out of the land of Egypt, my covenant that
they broke, though I was their husband, declares the Lord.
For this is the covenant that I will make with the house
of Israel after those days, declares the Lord:
I will put My law within them, and I will write it on
their hearts. And I will be their God, and they shall be
My people. And no longer shall each one teach his neigh-
bor and each his brother, saying, 'Know the Lord,' for they
shall all know Me, from the least of them to the greatest,
declares the Lord. For I will forgive their iniquity,
and I will remember their sin no more."

~ JEREMIAH 31: 31-34

Reflection:

I read the above text with the manger scene in my mind
and it's powerful! Christmas stands just two days away.

We'll see signs of the impending arrival everywhere as we go about our business today. We'll also likely have loads of "opportunities" to give our peace away in all the frenzy (note to self).

I cannot think about peace without thinking about the new covenant. This covenant makes possible my peace and yours. The forgiveness of sins and God's decision to put them out of His mind are gifts He offers to us. When we accept those gifts, we enter the new covenant with God. We are reconciled to Him, back in right standing and able to know Him as the prophet Jeremiah foretold. So peace is ours! It's ours to enjoy.

We are new covenant people at peace with our Maker because of all the Babe in the manger would do on our behalf! Wouldn't it be a shame to squander the peace that comes to us at so great a cost? Today let's not just protect and enjoy that peace, but be agents of peace for those in our path.

Response:

Lord, peace is such a coveted commodity. But You offer it to Your children in abundance. It's ours to enjoy and put on display. Come alive in me in the person of Your Spirit so that peace overrides any chaos today might bring. How often I have given my peace away, overwhelmed by the trappings of our cultural traditions surrounding Christmas. I ought to be the calm in the chaos! "You keep him in perfect peace, whose mind is stayed on You, because he trusts in You" (Isaiah 26:3). There's the answer! Thank You, Lord.

Remember:

_____

_____

_____

_____

_____

_____

_____

_____

_____

The Kingdom of God is Here

Peace Now and Forever

Meditation:

The Spirit of the Lord God is upon Me, because
the Lord has anointed Me to bring good news to the poor;
he has sent Me to bind up the brokenhearted,
to proclaim liberty to the captives,
and the opening of the prison to those who are bound;
to proclaim the year of the Lord's favor, and the day of
vengeance of our God; to comfort all who mourn;
to grant to those who mourn in Zion—
to give them a beautiful headdress instead of ashes,
the oil of gladness instead of mourning,
the garment of praise instead of a faint spirit.
They shall build up the ancient ruins;
they shall raise up the former devastations;
they shall repair the ruined cities,
the devastations of many generations.

~ ISAIAH 61:1–4

"The kingdom of God is not coming in ways
that can be observed,
nor will they say, 'Look, here it is!' or 'There!'
for behold, the kingdom of God is in the midst of you."

~ LUKE 17:20–21

Reflection:

Merry Christmas Eve, everyone! Thank you for traveling along with me these past weeks. I sincerely pray that you have been hearing from God and that these devotionals have helped that "hearing" to happen. Our final thought today is one that requires us to zoom out from the manger and look down upon the earth from high above it. Why? Because when Jesus came to earth as an infant, His Kingdom came with Him.

We absolutely cannot separate the Christmas story from the arrival of the Kingdom of God. And yet, we grapple daily with the fact that the Kingdom has not yet fully come. I've heard many preachers say that the Kingdom already present is really a kingdom within a kingdom. We are meant to live out the ethics of the Kingdom of God in the midst of the world's opposing kingdom. We're supposed to be displaying the values and behavior that will be the norm when Christ returns—all of which will appear radically abnormal until then.

And I think that's where we stop to ponder and pray. Tomorrow is Christmas. How can you and I live as if the Kingdom of God has already come? Because it has. When you get up tomorrow morning to commence with your traditions, how will you live differently as a citizen of the Kingdom of God? We might begin by reciting the words first offered from the mouth of the mother of Jesus. They are as true for us as they were for her: "My soul magnifies the Lord, and my spirit rejoices in God my Savior, for He who is mighty has done great things for me, and holy is His name" (Luke 1:47-49). That's a pretty powerful opening line to begin the celebration of the arrival of the Promised One!

May HOPE, FAITH, JOY and the PEACE of God abound in you and in those you love today and in the days to come. Merry Christmas, everyone!

Response:

Lord, I bow in reverence before You… my soul magnifies You! I celebrate You Emmanuel… God with us. I worship You, King of kings and Lord of lords. I exalt You, Savior of the world. I join the heavenly hosts and my brothers and sisters all around the world to celebrate the day that You came to the earth as a Baby. Be glorified today and every day! All praise and honor and glory is Yours, forever!

Remember:

_____

_____

_____

_____

Yea, Lord, we greet Thee,

born this happy morning;

Jesus, to Thee be all glory giv'n;

Word of the Father, now in flesh appearing.

O come let us adore Him

O come let us adore Him

O come let us adore Him

Christ the Lord!

JOHN FRANCIS WADE

(translated by Frederick Oakeley)

Anne Barbour

A NNE BARBOUR has been a guest speaker in both church and conference settings all over the nation including the Billy Graham Schools of Evangelism, The Billy Graham Training Center, and various women's conferences.

Anne writes a wide range of conference material that help women find and maintain a core connect with God so that He might do in and through them all that He intends. She also maintains a blog she describes as "musings and mutterings" about walking with God.

In 2017 Anne retired from an 11-year tenure at Hillcrest Christian School in Thousand Oaks, California. She was Chapel Head, providing direction and leadership for weekly chapels. She led Staff in their Spiritual Enrichment/Staff Inservice Days and taught a middle school and high school worship band.

Anne has also been active in the arena of contemporary worship as a singer and songwriter for 35 years. She was a founding member of the Maranatha Praise Band, now the

Tommy Coomes Band, and has traveled the world leading worship on platforms for Billy Graham, Franklin Graham, Chosen Women, Harvest Crusades, Anne Graham Lotz, Jill Briscoe, and many others. She has developed and led workshops on worship and songwriting throughout the country as part of the Tommy Coomes Band.

Anne and her husband John travel extensively leading worship and ministering in churches and conference centers. They have recorded seven CD's of their own and have fifteen as part of the Tommy Coomes Band. Anne has a solo project entitled, The Story of Perfect Love, designed as a catalyst for personal worship. Anne has also been a studio musician for the past 30 years recording for television, radio, and various recording artists.

Anne lives in Newbury Park, CA with her husband John. They have one grown son named Evan.

For information, blog, bookings, and product visit:

annebarbour.com

Gifts For The Christ Child

The following pages are for you to either write or draw on. The greatest gift we can offer God is the gift of ourselves. As He has gifted us with Himself, how appropriate that we respond in kind. What would you say to the Christ Child that might be a gift to Him? What would you draw that would reflect your heart of gratitude for who He is and for all He has done for you?

They fell down and worshiped Him.
Then, opening their treasures,
they offered Him gifts.

~ MATTHEW 2:11